DAO DE JING
IN CLEAR ENGLISH

POCKET EDITION

Dao De Jing
in Clear English

Pocket Edition

by Laozi

Translation and Commentary by
Jeff Pepper and Xiao Hui Wang

IMAGIN8
PRESS

Cover and book design by Jeff Pepper
Artwork by Next Mars Media, Luoyang, China

Photo Credits:

- Page 105, Figure 1 (Laozi statue): Photo source: Thanato (own work) CC BY-SA 3.0 (https://creativecommons.org/licenses/by- sa/3.0), via Wikimedia Commons.
- Page 106 (Figure 2: Guodian slips): Original in Hubei Provincial Museum. Photo source: By Sharkman (own work), CC BY-SA 3.0

Typeset in Adobe Garamond (body) and Senty Wen (Chinese calligraphy)

ISBN: 978-1732063815

Version 05a

ACKNOWLEDGEMENTS

We are deeply indebted to the many scholars who have labored to uncover, translate and interpret the Dao De Jing. We especially want to thank Dr. Bruce R. Linnell, whose *Minimalist Translation of the Dao De Jing by Lao Zi* (Gutenberg Project, 2015) was so helpful to us in this project. Translations that were particularly helpful were *Dao De Jing: The Book of the Way* (Moss Roberts, University of California Press, 2004), *Dao De Jing: A Philosophical Translation* (Roger Ames and David Hall, Ballantine Books, 2003), and the beautifully written and illustrated *Tao Te Ching* (Gia-Fu Feng and Jane English, Vintage Book, 1972). When we needed help with the original text, we often relied on the Chinese-language book 道德经 (Dao De Jing), annotated by Li Yan Wang (China Federation of Literary and Art Circles Publishing Corp, 2017). We are also grateful for the many online research tools listed in the Resources section at the end of this book.

Finally, we owe a debt of gratitude to William David Hetzel for his thorough review of the manuscript. And for their deep insights and thoughtful analysis of each chapter of the Dao De Jing, we can't say enough about the contributions from the members of the Dao Bums online discussion group www.thedaobums.com.

Of course, we take full responsibility for any and all errors. Please feel free to let us know if you find any, you can reach us at info@imagin8press.com.

ABOUT THIS BOOK

The book that you are reading contains the completion translation of the Dao De Jing. However, if you are interested in learning more about the original Dao De Jing and how its 2500-year-old text is translated into modern English, we recommend the longer version of this book: *Dao De Jing in Clear English, Including a Step by Step Translation* (Imagin8 Press, 2018).

That book contains the same translation that you will read here. But we also show each chapter in the original Chinese, then in pinyin (phonetic spelling using English letters), then a word-by-word literal translation, and then any notes that we feel would help you understand the text.

WELCOME!

The eighty-one chapters of this book are like tasty
morsels, set out carefully on a long buffet table.
Candles are flickering. You have been invited to be an
honored guest.

Come on in. Take a bite, chew it slowly. Try to taste
all the flavors.

Later on, maybe take another bite or two.

No need to eat too much at once!

The Dao is the way of balance and harmony.

Part 1: Dao Jing

1

The Dao that can be spoken is not the eternal Dao.

The name that can be named is not the eternal name.

Nameless, the beginning of heaven and earth.

Named, the mother of ten thousand things.

Being empty, see the wonder.

Being present, see the appearance.

These two are the same but have different names,

This is mystery.

Mystery upon mystery,

The doorway to wonder.

2

In this world, beauty is called beauty because there is ugliness.

Good is called good because there is evil.

Thus, emptiness and existence transform into each other,

Difficult and easy come from each other,

Long and short compare to each other,

High and low flow from each other,

Sounds and voices blend together in harmony,

Before and after follow each other.

Knowing this, the sage acts by doing nothing,

And teaches without saying a word.

The ten thousand things arise but he is silent.

Things grow but he takes nothing for himself.

He acts but doesn't compel.

He creates but seeks no recognition.

By not seeking recognition, he has nothing to lose.

3

Don't honor good men, and the people will not strive.

Don't value rare goods, and the people will not steal.

Don't show off valuables, and the peoples' hearts will not be confused.

Thus, the wise ruler empties minds and fills stomachs,

Weakens ambitions and strengthens bones.

Make sure the people have no knowledge and no desire.

Those who have knowledge will not dare to act!

Do without doing, and all will be peaceful.

4

Dao is a bottomless cup that need not be filled.

Profound and deep, it is the root of ten thousand things.

It blunts sharpness, loosens tangles,

Softens brightness, makes us as dust.

Deep and profound! It barely exists.

I don't know whose child it is.

It appeared before the great kings.

5

Heaven and earth aren't kind;

To them, the ten thousand things are as straw dogs.

The sage isn't kind;

To him, the common people are as straw dogs.

Isn't the space between heaven and earth like a bellows?

It is empty but cannot be exhausted.

The more it moves, the more comes out.

The more you talk, the weaker you become.

Better to remain centered.

6

The spirit of the center is called the mysterious feminine.

Its doorway is called the source of heaven and earth.

It seems to be unbroken.

Use it; it never ends.

7

Heaven is eternal, earth lasts a long time,

So heaven and earth can last forever.

They don't live for themselves,

So they can live a long time.

Thus, the sage puts himself behind,

Yet finds himself in front.

Giving no thought for himself,

He survives.

Is it because he is selfless

That he can achieve selfish goals?

8

The highest kindness is like water.

Water's kindness benefits everything, yet it doesn't strive.

It even lives in places that everyone dislikes, like the Dao.

The virtue of a home is its land,

The virtue of the heart is its depth,

The virtue of a friendship is its kindness,

The virtue of speech is its honesty,

The virtue of governing is establishing peaceful order,

The virtue of doing your duty is being competent,

The virtue of action is its timing.

When there is no striving, there is no blame.

9

Filling up isn't as good as knowing when to stop.

A sharp point can't be maintained for long.

When gold and jade fill a room, no one can protect it.

When wealth leads to arrogance, it invites mistakes.

Achieve success, then let it go.

This is the Dao of heaven.

10

The body embraces the soul,

Can you not split them apart?

Concentrate the breath to become soft,

Can you be like a newborn infant?
Purify and examine your deepest thoughts,

Can you be without blemish?

Love the citizens and govern the nation,

Can you do nothing?

Open your senses to meet the world,

Can you remain calm?

See clearly in all four directions,

Can you not interfere?

Create and nurture,

Create but don't possess,

Act but don't compel,

Lead but don't dominate.

This is called the mysterious De.

11

Thirty spokes share a single hub,

Its emptiness makes the cart useful.

Form clay to make a container,

Its emptiness makes the container useful.

Cut doors and windows to make a room,

Its emptiness makes the room useful.

So, a thing's existence makes it beneficial,

But emptiness makes it useful.

12

The five colors can make our eyes blind.

The five tones can make our ears deaf.
The five flavors can make our mouths dull.

Horse racing and hunting can make our hearts go
mad.

Rare goods can make us corrupt.

So, the sage feeds the people

And doesn't distract them.

He leaves that and chooses this.

13

Favor and humiliation are both frightening.

Pay attention to risk as you would to your own body.

Why do we say "favor and humiliation are both
frightening"?

Favor makes you inferior.

You fear getting it and fear losing it.

This is the meaning of "favor and humiliation are both frightening".

Why do we say "pay attention to risk as you would to your own body"?

I suffer because I have a body.

If I have no body, how can I suffer?

If you can treat the world like your own body, take it.

If you can love the world like your own body, rule it.

14

Look but not see, call it dim.

Listen but not hear, call it faint.

Reach but not grasp, call it slight.

These three things can't be investigated, they blend and become one.

Its top is not bright, its bottom is not dark.

Unceasing, nameless, it returns to the void.

It is the form of the formless, the image of the void.

Confusing and indistinct.

Meet it, you can't see its beginning;

Follow it, you can't see its end.

Hold fast to the ancient Dao,

Master the present moment.

Know the ancient beginning,

Remain grounded in the Dao.

15

The ancient masters were subtle, deep, mysterious.

We can't understand their mysterious depths.
 We can't understand them,

But we must try to describe them.

Cautious, as if crossing a winter stream!

Watchful, as if afraid of threats from all sides!

Respectful, like a visiting guest!

Yielding, like the breakup of winter ice!

Simple and honest, like an uncarved block!

Wide and open, like a valley!

Murky, like muddy water!

Who can take muddy water, and through stillness make it clear?

Who can take what is tranquil, and through movement bring it to life?

Maintain the Dao, you won't want to be full.

If you're not full, there is no need to be renewed.

16

Become completely empty,

Maintain true stillness.

The ten thousand creatures all arise, and I watch them return,

Swarming, they return to their source.

Returning to the source is called stillness,

It's called returning to nature,

Returning to nature is called unchanging,

Knowing the unchanging is called insight.

Not knowing the unchanging is reckless and leads to misfortune.

Knowing the unchanging leads to tolerance.

Tolerance leads to justice,

Justice leads to royalty,

Royalty leads to Heaven,

Heaven leads to Dao,

Dao leads to eternity.

All your life, you're in no danger.

17

The greatest ruler is barely known to the people.

Next, one who is loved.

Next, one who is feared.

Next, one who is ridiculed.

If the ruler doesn't trust, then the people will have no trust.

Relaxed, he rarely gives orders!

When tasks are completed and duties fulfilled,

The common people all say, "This is our natural way."

18

When natural order is abandoned,

There is kindness and morality.

When intelligence and intellect appear,

There is great deception.

When the six kinships are not in harmony,

Children show piety to their parents.

When nations and families fall into darkness and confusion,

There are loyal ministers.

19

Renounce holiness, abandon cleverness,

And the people benefit a hundredfold.

Renounce morality, abandon ethics,

And the people return to being kind and devoted children.

Renounce cleverness, abandon profit,

And thieves won't exist.

These three make a civil society, but it isn't enough.

So we must let people believe in these:

Maintain simplicity, embrace plainness.

Less selfishness, fewer desires.

20

Renounce learning, avoid suffering.

How far apart are "yes" and "yeah"?

How similar are good and evil?

Should we fear what others fear?

It's been like this since ancient times, it never ends.

Crowds of people are excited,

As if going to the sacrifice feast,

As if climbing terraces in the spring.

I alone am still and give no sign.

Like a newborn infant not yet a child.

So tired, with nowhere to return to!

Everyone has more than they need; but I have nothing.

So confused! I have the heart of a fool.

Common people see clearly; I alone am dazed.

Common people look sharply; I alone am simple.

They are boundless like the sea, and endless like the wind.

Everyone is shrewd; I alone am clumsy.

I alone am different from the people,

Because I value the mother of all.

21

The greatest De is possible only by following the Dao.

Dao is indistinct and blurry.

Blurry and indistinct! Inside is appearance.

Indistinct and blurry! Inside are things.

Obscure and dark! Inside is essence.

Its essence is truth. Inside is trust.

Since ancient times its name is not lost,

So I see the ancestor of the many.

How do I know this is the ancestor of the many?

Through this.

22

Yielding brings wholeness,

Bending brings straightness,

Emptying brings fullness,

Decaying brings renewal,

Diminishing brings gain,

Exceeding brings confusion.

Thus the sage embraces the One

And serves as an example to the world.

He doesn't display himself, so he appears.

He doesn't promote himself, so he succeeds.

He doesn't boast, so he becomes famous.

He doesn't brag, so he remains a long time.

Because he doesn't fight,

No one under heaven can fight against him.

The ancients say: those who yield become whole.

How can these words be wrong?

True wholeness will return to you.

23

Nature's words are few.

So, strong winds don't last the entire morning,

Sudden rains don't last all day.

Who makes these things? Heaven and earth.

Even heaven and earth can't maintain them forever,

So how can people do it?

So, engage with Dao, and become one with Dao.

Engage with De, and become one with De.

Engage with loss, and become one with loss.

Become one with Dao, and Dao welcomes you.

Become one with De, and De welcomes you.

Become one with loss, and loss welcomes you.

If you aren't worthy of trust, others won't trust you.

24

One who stands on tiptoe doesn't really stand.

One who strides doesn't really walk.

One who is narrowminded doesn't have a clear view.

One who is self-righteous misses the obvious.

One who boasts doesn't achieve.

One who brags doesn't endure.

One who lives in Dao calls these

Leftover food, big belly.

People don't like them.

So, one who has Dao avoids them.

25

Something formless appeared,

Before the birth of heaven and earth.

Quiet! Sparse!

It stands alone, unchanging.

It moves everywhere endlessly,

It could be the mother of the world.

I don't know its name;

Its symbol is Dao.

If I had to name it, I would call it great.

Greatness speaks of departure.

Departure speaks of distance.

Distance speaks of returning.

Dao is great, Heaven is great,

Earth is great, the king is also great.

In this land are four great ones,

And the king is one of them!

People obey earth,

Earth obeys heaven,

Heaven obeys Dao,

Dao obeys what is natural.

26

Heavy is the source of light,

Stillness is the master of impatience.

So, the sage travels all day,

And never leaves his supply wagon.

Despite glorious sights, the sage lives apart.

This is how he transcends them.

How can the master of ten thousand chariots

Act lightly in public?

Act lightly, lose the source.

Act with haste, lose the throne.

27

A good traveler leaves no tracks.

A good speaker is without flaw or disgrace.

A good accountant needs no counting tokens.

A good door has no bolt, but it can't be opened.

A good binding has no rope, but it can't be loosened.

Thus the sage always rescues people, so no one is
abandoned.

The sage always preserves things, so nothing is
abandoned.

This is called innate wisdom.

So, a good person is the teacher of a bad one,

And a bad person is a lesson for a good one.

If no respect for the teacher, then no care for the lesson.

Even with wisdom there is great confusion.

This is called the essence of mystery.

28

Know the male but maintain the female.

Be a mountain stream in the world.

Be a mountain stream.

The constant De will remain,

Returning you to being a newborn.

Know the bright but maintain the dark.

Be an example in the world.

Be an example.

The constant De will not fail,

It will return you to being limitless.

Know your honor but maintain your disgrace.

Be a valley in the world.

Be a valley.

The constant De will satisfy.

Returning you to simplicity.

When the simple comes apart,

The sage uses it as a tool.

He becomes a public servant,
And great systems are not shattered.

29

Take the world and control it?

I don't see how it can be done.

The world is a marvel,

You can't control it.

Act, and you ruin it,

Grasp, and you lose it.

So, creatures can lead or follow,

Can breathe shallow or deep,

Can be strong or weak,

Can be kept down or rise up.

So, the sage

Abandons overdoing, wastefulness, and pride.

30

Use Dao to assist the lords of the people,

But don't use military force,

For there will be retribution.

Where armies camp, thorns grow.

After armies leave, the harvest is poor.

The wise person gets results, then stops.

He doesn't dare to take by force.

Results without bragging,

Results without boasting,

Results without arrogance,

Results only as a last resort,

Results without a show of strength.

Creatures grow strong, then age.

This is called not Dao.

Not Dao soon ends.

31

Fine weapons are tools of misfortune.

People hate them.

So, one who has Dao does not live by them.

The nobleman usually honors the left,

But when he commands troops, he honors the right.

Weapons are tools of misfortune,

They are not the tools of a nobleman.

When using them, it's best to be restrained.

If you are victorious, don't embrace it.

If you embrace it, you enjoy killing people.

One who enjoys killing people

Can't get what he wants in the world!

Good things always on the left,

Bad things always on the right.

The lieutenant general stands on the left,

The general stands on the right.

Treat it like a funeral ceremony.

Many people are killed,

Pitiful cries of sorrow,

Victory in war should be treated like a funeral ceremony.

32

Dao is forever nameless.

Even though it's simple and small,

In this world it can't be conquered!

If lords and kings could maintain it,

The ten thousand creatures would submit.

Heaven and earth would join together,

And a sweet dew would fall.

No citizens would force this,

But it would naturally be in harmony.

In the beginning, it had a name.

Having a name, men would know when to stop.

Knowing when to stop, they avoid danger.

Dao in this world is like a stream in the valley,

Flowing into a river,

Into the sea.

33

Know people and you are wise,

Know yourself and you have insight.

Triumph over other people and you have influence,

Triumph over yourself and you are strong.

Know you have enough and you are rich,

Be determined and you will have a strong will.

Don't lose your place, and you will endure,

Die but don't be destroyed, and you will live forever.

34

Great Dao is like a flood!

It can flow left and right.

The ten thousand creatures depend on it for life,

It doesn't reject them.

It completes its tasks but takes no name.

It clothes and supports the ten thousand creatures,

But is not their master.

Having no desire,

It can be called insignificant.

The ten thousand creatures return, but it is not their master,

It can be called great.

In the end it doesn't make itself great,

And so it achieves greatness.

35

Holding the great image in its hands,

The whole world comes to it.

Come to it without hurting each other,

There is safety and peace.

Music and good food make guests stay,

But Dao's words come out weak and flavorless!

Look for it, you can't see it,

Listen for it, you can't hear it,

Use it, you can't exhaust it.

36

When you want to draw something in,

You must first stretch it out.

When you want to weaken something,

You must first make it strong.

When you want to abandon something,

You must first promote it.

When you want to seize something,

You must first give it something.

This is subtle wisdom.

Soft and weak conquers hard and strong,

Fish can't escape from deep waters.

The sharp tools of the nation

Can't be shown to the people.

37

Dao does nothing,

Yet nothing is left undone.

If lords and kings could grasp this,

The ten thousand creatures would transform
themselves.

If transformation leads to desire,

I will suppress it by using nameless simplicity.

Nameless simplicity eliminates desire.

Without desire, all is peaceful,

And the world settles itself.

Part 2: De Jing

德经

38

One with high De has no De, and so truly has De.

One with low De never loses De, and so truly has no De.

One with high De does nothing and has no selfish motives.

One with low De acts and has selfish motives.

A kind person acts and has no selfish motives.

A moral person acts and has selfish motives.

A well-mannered person acts, but no one responds,

They roll up their sleeves and force others to respond.

Lose Dao and you have De,

Lose De and you have kindness,

Lose kindness and you have morality.

Lose morality and you have good behavior.

Good behavior looks like loyalty and honesty,

But it's the beginning of confusion.

Wise people have crazy ideas about Dao,

That's the beginning of foolishness.

So, the sage

Lives by the substantial, not the weak,

Lives by the truth, not crazy ideas.

He leaves that and choose this.

39

Ancients who have attained oneness:

The sky attained oneness and became clear.

Earth attained oneness and became peaceful,

The gods attained oneness and became divine,

The valley attained oneness and became full,

The ten thousand creatures attained oneness and flourished,

Lords and kings attained oneness and became leaders.

In other words,

If the sky were not clear, I'm afraid it would break apart.

If earth were not peaceful, I'm afraid it would erupt.

If the gods were not wise, I'm afraid they would disappear.

If the valley were not full, I'm afraid it would be used up.

If the ten thousand creatures were not growing, I'm afraid they would be wiped out.

If lords and kings were not high up, I'm afraid they would fall.

High rank has its origin in low value,

The high has its foundation in the low.

Thus lords and kings call themselves orphaned, lonely, and hungry.

Isn't this because the root of high rank is low value?

Isn't it?

Many honors is the same as no honor.

Don't desire to be precious like jade,

Be common like rock.

40

The motion of Dao is to return.

The function of Dao is to weaken.

The ten thousand creatures of the world are born from being;

Being is born from non-being.

41

The highest student of Dao practices it diligently.

The middle student of Dao is unsure.

The lowest student of Dao laughs out loud.

Without laughter, there's no Dao.

So, it is said:

The brightest Dao seems like darkness,

The boldest Dao seems like retreating,

The smoothest Dao seems to be knotted,

The highest De seems like a valley,

The whitest things seem muddy,

The broadest De seems incomplete,

The newest De seems slow,

The purest things seem murky,

The squarest things have no corners,

The greatest tools are completed last,

The greatest tones are inaudible,

The greatest images have no form,

Dao is hidden and has no name.

So, only Dao is good at giving and accomplishing.

42

Dao gives birth to one,

One gives birth to two,

Two gives birth to three,

Three gives birth to the ten thousand creatures.

The ten thousand creatures carry Yin and embrace Yang,

Flowing together in harmony.

People hate being orphaned, lonely, and hungry,

Yet this is what kings and lords call themselves.

So, creatures

Sometimes weaken but then gain strength,

Sometimes strengthen but then grow weak.

I teach what others have taught.

Hoodlums don't die a natural death.

This is the basis of my teaching.

43

The softest things in the world

Overrun the hardest things.

The formless enters where there is no gap.

And so I know the benefits of not doing.

Teaching without words,

The benefit of doing nothing,

Few in the world can match this.

44

Fame or life: which do you prefer?

Life or property: which is more precious?

Gain or loss: which is more harmful?

Great desire brings great cost.

Much gathering brings much loss.

Know when you have enough, there's no disgrace.

Know when you have to stop, there's no danger.

And so you can live a long time.

45

Great achievement can appear incomplete,

Use it, it won't fail.

Great fullness can appear empty,

Use it, it won't run dry.

Great straightness can appear bent.

Great skill can appear clumsy.

Great eloquence can sound like stammering.

Movement can conquer cold,

Stillness can conquer heat.

Serenity keeps the world in order.

46

When the world has Dao,

Riding horses work in the fields.

When the world has no Dao,

War horses give birth in the countryside.

No crime is greater than the feeling of desire.

No misfortune is greater than not knowing when
enough is enough.

No fault is greater than wanting more and more.

So, know when enough is enough.
There is always enough!

47

Without going out the door

You can still understand the world.

Without looking out the window

You can still know the Dao of heaven.

The further you go

The less you know.

So, the sage doesn't travel, yet knows.

Doesn't show off, yet is famous.

Doesn't act, yet accomplishes.

48

For those who study, more every day.

For those who practice Dao, less every day.

Less and less,

Until you arrive at doing nothing.

Do nothing, and nothing is left undone.

To conquer the world, just do nothing.

If you must do things,

You can't conquer the world.

49

The sage doesn't maintain his own heart,

So the common peoples' hearts become his heart.

If someone is good to me, I am good to him,

If someone is not good to me, I am still good to him,

Because De is good.

If someone is honest with me, I am honest with them,

If someone is not honest with me, I am still honest with him,

Because De is honesty.

The sage lives in the world, draws it all in,

And lets all their hearts become simple and honest.

The common people all focus on what they hear and see.

The sage has restored them to being like children.

50

From beginning life to entering death,

Followers of life are three in ten,

Followers of death are three in ten,

Those who drift towards their places of death, three in ten.

Why?

Because they live for life's sensations.

It's said that one who cares intensely for life

Can travel the land and not meet rhinos or tigers,

Can enter battle without shield or sword.

The rhino has no place to thrust its horn,

The tiger has no place to use its claws,

The soldier's blade has no place to enter.

Why?

Because in him there is no place for death.

51

Dao gives birth to them,

De raises them,

They begin to take shape,

Circumstances complete them.

So, of the ten thousand creatures

None fail to respect Dao, and they honor De.

Respecting Dao,

Honoring De.

This is not commanded,

But is the natural way of things.

So, Dao gives life to them,

De raises them, grows them, nourishes them,

Shelters and heals them,

Supports and protects them,

Gives them birth but doesn't own them,

Acts but doesn't care about results,

Leads them but doesn't control them.

This is called Primal De.

52

The world had a beginning,

This was the mother of the world.

When you find the mother,

You know her children.

Once you know her children,

You return to and stand with their mother.

All your life, you're in no danger.

Block your senses, shut the gates,

All your life, you won't work hard.

Open your senses, immerse yourself in your affairs,

All your life, you won't be rescued.

Seeing the small is called insight,

Maintaining the soft is called strength.

Use the light and come back to your insight.

Stay out of trouble and practice your normal routine.

53

If I have a little knowledge

While walking the great road,

I fear I might wander off.

The great road is very smooth,

But people like the side paths.

The royal court is well swept.

The fields are overgrown with weeds,

And the granaries are completely empty.

They wear colorful silks,

Carry sharp swords,

They stuff themselves with drink and food,

And have a surplus of riches.

This is called robbery and extravagance,

Not Dao!

54

Well established things are not easily uprooted.

Well held things are not easily pulled away.

That's why children and grandchildren continue to offer sacrifices.

Cultivate yourself, your De will be true.

Cultivate your family, its De will be enough.

Cultivate your village, its De will be long-lived.

Cultivate your nation, its De will be abundant.

Cultivate your world, its De will be everywhere.

So, use yourself to know yourself.

Use your family to know your family.

Use the village to know the village.

Use the nation to know the nation.

Use the world to know the world.

How do I know the world is like this?

Because of this.

55

One who holds the essence of De

Is like a newborn baby.

Wasps, scorpions and snakes don't sting him,

Savage beasts don't claw him,

Birds of prey do don't not seize him.

His bones are weak, his muscles are soft, but his grip is strong.

He has not yet known the union of female and male, yet he is erect.

His manhood is great!

He wails all day but doesn't get hoarse.

His harmony is great!

Knowing harmony is called unchanging,

Knowing the unchanging is called wisdom,

Trying to improve your life is called bad fortune.

Trying to control the Qi with your mind is called foolish strength.

Creatures grow strong, then age.

This is called not Dao.

Not Dao soon ends.

56

He who knows doesn't speak,

He who speaks doesn't know.

Block your senses, shut the gates,

Blunt your sharpness,

Unravel your tangles,

Soften your brightness,

Be the same as dust.

This is called a deep sameness.

So, you can't have it and be intimate,

You can't have it and stand apart.

You can't have it and benefit,

You can't have it and cause harm,

You can't have it and be noble,

You can't have it and be worthless.

So, in the world you will lead.

57

Use justice when governing a nation,

Use surprise tactics when commanding troops,

Use no striving to capture the world.

How do I know this?

Because of this:

The more fears and taboos there are in the world,

The poorer the citizens become.

The more sharp weapons the citizens have,

The more nations and families fall into darkness.
The more talented and clever the people are,

The more unexplained things happen.

The more new laws are proclaimed,

The more bandits there are.

So, the sage says:

I do not act, and the citizens begin to obey.

I enjoy peace, and the citizens become just.

I do nothing, and the citizens become wealthy.

I have no desire, and the citizens become simple and honest.

58

If government doesn't interfere,

Its citizens will be very simple and honest.

If government is very suspicious,
Its citizens will be very dissatisfied.

Disaster! It is rooted in good fortune.

Good fortune! It lies hidden in disaster.

Who knows its reach?

Nobody knows.

Justice becomes evil,

Goodness also becomes evil.

The people have been bewitched for a long time.

Thus, the sage is

Honest but not critical,

Strong but not hurtful,

Straightforward but not pushy,

Brilliant but not shiny.

59

Whether governing people or serving heaven,

Be like a farmer who stores rice.

Storing your rice is called preparing early.

Preparing early is called accumulating De.

Accumulate De, and everything can be overcome.

When everything can be overcome, there are no limits.

When there are no limits, you can have the nation.

When you have the mother of the nation, you can last a long time.

This is called having deep roots and firm ground,

The Dao of long life and lasting vision.

60

Governing a great nation is like cooking a small fish.

Because Dao has come into the world,

Death and decay have no spiritual power.

Not that death and decay have no spiritual power,

But its spiritual power doesn't hurt people.

Not only does its spiritual power not hurt people,

The sage also doesn't hurt people.

These two don't hurt each other,

Therefore De returns!

61

A great nation is the valley to which all waters flow,

The confluence of the world,

The female of the world.

The female uses stillness to conquer the male,

She uses stillness to remain low.

So, a great nation becomes lower than a small nation,

And thus wins over the small nation.

A small nation becomes lower than a great nation,

And thus is won over by the great nation.

So, some become low to win over,

Some become low to be won over.

A great nation doesn't want to be too controlling,

A small nation doesn't want to be too submissive.

So, for both nations to get what they want,

The great nation should remain low.

62

Dao is the deep mystery of the ten thousand things,

Treasure for a person with virtue,

Protection for a person without virtue.

Use pretty words to become popular,

Use good deeds to win respect,

But how can those without virtue give up on it?

So, when installing the emperor on his throne,

Or appointing the three nobles,

You can offer jade disks and horse-drawn carriages,
But it's not as good as sitting and entering the Dao.

Why did the ancients value the Dao so highly?

Didn't they say,

Seek and you will find it,

And your crimes will be erased?

Thus, Dao becomes valuable to the world.

63

Act without acting,

Work without getting involved,

Taste without tasting.

No matter how great or how often,

Repay injury with De.

Overcome the hard while it is still easy,
Achieve the large while it is still tiny.

The world's difficult things surely begin easy.

The world's great things surely begin tiny.

Therefore, the sage in the end sees nothing as great,

And so can accomplish great things.

Make promises lightly and few will trust you.

Expect things to be easy and they will be difficult.

Therefore, the sage sees everything as difficult,

So in the end nothing is difficult!

64

Things at rest are easy to hold,

Things not yet been revealed are easy to plan for,

Brittle things are easily shattered,
Small things are easily scattered.

Deal with things before they appear,

Set things in order before they are in chaos.

A tree too big to embrace is born from a tiny shoot.

A tower of nine stories rises from a heap of dirt.

A journey of a thousand miles begins with a single step.

Act and you'll be defeated,

Grasp and you'll lose.

Thus the sage

Doesn't act, so he is not defeated,

Doesn't grasp, so he doesn't lose.

People often fail when they've almost completed their tasks.

So, be as careful at the end as in the beginning,

Then you will not ruin your affairs.

Thus the sage:

Pursues what others don't pursue,

Has no interest in rare goods,

Learns what others don't learn,

Corrects the mistakes of others,

Helps the ten thousand creatures to what is natural,

But doesn't dare to act.

65

The ancients acted in Dao,

Not to give the citizens knowledge,

But to let them become simple.

Citizens are hard to govern

When they have too much knowledge.

So, using knowledge to govern the nation is thievery.

Not using knowledge to govern the nation is good fortune.

Understand these two and use them as principles.

Always understand these principles,

This is called Primal De.

Primal De is deep and everlasting!

When creatures return,

They reach their greatest harmony.

66

Rivers and seas can be kings of the hundred valleys,

Because they are good at lying low,

And so, they can be kings of the hundred valleys.

So, if the sage wants to be above the citizens,

He must speak as if he is lower than them.

If the sage wants to be in front of the citizens,

He must follow behind them.

Thus the sage

Lives above them, but the citizens aren't burdened.

Lives in front of them, but the citizens aren't harmed.

The world will support him, and won't tire of him.

He doesn't strive,

So no one in the world can strive against him.

67

Everyone in the world says my Dao is great,

But it's like nothing else.

The reason it's great is because it's like nothing else.

If it was like everything else all this time,

It would be insignificant!

Now I have three treasures that I hold and protect:

The first is compassion,

The second is frugality,

The third is not daring to be in front.

Because I'm kind I can be brave.

Because I'm frugal I can be generous.

Because I'm not in front, I can lead others.

Today, people abandon kindness, trying to be brave.

Abandon frugality, trying to be generous.

Abandon following, trying to be in front.

This is death!

Kindness in battle brings victory,

In defense it brings strength.

Heaven will rescue you,

And with kindness protect you.

68

A good commander is not fierce.

A good warrior is not angry.

A good conqueror doesn't engage the enemy.

A good leader serves from below.

This is called the De of not striving.

This is called the power of leadership.

This is called matching Heaven's ancient way.

69

The masters of war have a saying:

I dare not act like the host, but instead act like a guest.

I dare not advance an inch, but instead retreat a foot.

This is called advancing without advancing,

Striking without using your arms,

Attacking without enemies,

Defending without soldiers.

Nothing is worse than underestimating the enemy.

Underestimating the enemy, I nearly lost my treasures.
So, when opposing armies come together,

The merciful side will be victorious!

70

My words are very easy to understand,

Very easy to practice.

In this world, they can't be understood,

And can't be practiced.

My words have ancestors,

My duties have rulers.

So because people don't understand,

They think I don't understand.

Few people understand me.

They are very valuable!

So, the sage wears rough clothing,

But carries jade in his heart.

71

Knowing that you are ignorant is best,

Being ignorant but thinking that you know is a sickness.

Only when you see sickness as sickness,

Can you be healthy.

The sage is healthy

Because he knows sickness as sickness.

Therefore he is healthy.

72

If the citizens don't respect power,

Then a greater power will arrive!

Don't disrupt their homes,

Don't despise their lives.

Don't despise them,

And they won't despise you.

Thus the sage

Knows himself but doesn't show off,

Loves himself but isn't arrogant,

Leaves that and chooses this.

73

Courage in daring brings death,

Courage in not daring brings life.

Of these two, one is helpful and the other harmful.

When heaven brings failure, who knows its reasons?

The Dao of heaven doesn't strive, but skillfully wins,

Doesn't speak, but skillfully answers,

Doesn't call, but comes itself,

Doesn't hurry, but skillfully prepares.

Heaven's net is extremely vast,

Its mesh is wide but it doesn't fail.

74

If citizens don't fear death,

Why threaten them with death?

If I could make citizens fear death,

Then I could seize those who act strange and kill them,

And then who would dare?

There will always be an executioner.

The executioner is like a master carpenter carving wood.

One who takes the place of a master carpenter to carve wood,

Won't escape cutting their own hands!

75

The citizens are hungry,

Because their superiors take too much of their food.

That's why they are hungry.

The citizens are hard to rule,

Because their superiors are compelled to act.

That's why they are hard to rule.

The citizens take death lightly,

Because their superiors pursue the rich things in life.

Thus they take death lightly.

Thus, those who act without concern for life,

Are worth more than those who highly value life.

76

People are born soft and weak,

They die hard and strong.

All creatures, grass and trees are born soft and fragile,

They die dry and withered.

Hard and strong are disciples of death,

Soft and weak are disciples of life.

An unyielding army is defeated,

An unbending tree is ready to fall.

Big and strong dwell below,

Soft and flexible dwell above.

77

The Dao of heaven, how it is like bending a bow?

That which is high, press it down.

That which is low, raise it up.

That which has too much, take away.

That which has not enough, add more.

The Dao of heaven

Reduces that which has too much,

Fills that which has too little.

The way of people isn't like this,

It takes from that which has too little,

And offers it to that which has too much.

Who can have too much and then offer it to the world?

Only one who has Dao.

Thus the sage

Acts, but does not compel,

Accomplishes tasks, but doesn't dwell on them,

And has no desire to show off worth.

78

In this world nothing is softer and weaker than water,

Yet for attacking that which is hard and strong,

Nothing can surpass it,

Nothing can replace it.

Weak is better than strong,

Flexible is better than hard.

In this world,
None fails to comprehend this,

None can practice it.

Thus the sage says:

Taking on the dirt of the nation

Is called being the master of the altars of field and grains.

Taking on the misfortune of the nation

Is called being king of the world.

Straight talk may seem contrary.

79

Reconcile a great grievance,

And there will certainly be lingering grievances.

How can this be good?

Thus the sage

Holds the left side of a contract,

But makes no demands of people.

Having De, look after your obligations,

Without De, look after your claims on others.

The Dao of heaven has no favorites,

But it favors good people.

80

In a small nation with few citizens,

It has the weapons of a hundred men,

But doesn't use them.

The citizens take death seriously, but they don't travel far.
They have boats and carts, but they don't need to ride them.

They have armor and weapons, but they don't need to display them.

Let the citizens return to using knotted cords,

Finding sweetness in their food,

Beauty in their clothes,

Contentment in their homes,

Enjoyment in their customs.

Other nations can be seen nearby,

Sounds of chickens and dogs can be heard,

But the citizens reach old age and die,

Without traveling far to visit each other.

81

True words aren't pretty,

Pretty words aren't true.

One who is good doesn't argue,

One who argues isn't good.

One who knows doesn't boast,

One who boasts doesn't know.

The sage doesn't accumulate,

But by serving people, gains even more.

By giving to people, has even more.

The Dao of heaven transforms but doesn't harm.

The Dao of the sage acts but doesn't strive.

Translators' Notes

There are hundreds of translations of the Dao De Jing[1], which we'll abbreviate as DDJ from here on. They all follow a similar format: they begin with detailed notes written by the translator that discuss the book, its underlying philosophy, and the translation process, and that's followed by the translated text itself. As you see, we've taken the opposite approach: the DDJ comes first, and here at the end we'll just give you some brief notes.

When we say "brief", we're not kidding. We'll start off with a little bit of history of the DDJ itself, then talk about how we approached this translation project, and give you some tips on how you can best use this book.

However, if you're looking for a detailed discussion on Daoism, you'll have to look elsewhere. There are many excellent books on Daoism, but we prefer not to talk very much about that. Our single goal is to give you the DDJ, the whole DDJ, and nothing but the DDJ, in a clear style that's as close as possible to the original, and let you decide for yourself what the words mean.

---

[1] You may have seen this book called the *Tao Te Ching* or *Tao Teh Ching*. That was the name of the book in English until 1958, when the Chinese government replaced the old Wade-Giles sysem of romanizing Chinese proper names with new names that used pinyin spelling and correct pronounciation. So, for example, Peking became Beijing, and Mao Tse Tung became Mao Zedong. Thus, Tao became Dao, Taoism became Daoism, and the Tao Te Ching became the Dao De Jing.

People have spent over two thousand years trying to understand and interpret the DDJ. Now it's your turn to read the book and come up with your own understanding of its timeless wisdom.

道

Nobody really knows who wrote the DDJ.

A popular folk tale tells how it might have happened. A long time ago, China was not a unified country but just a patchwork of small feudal kingdoms constantly at war with each other. The people longed for a return to peace and order.

In the central plains of China, in the ancient capital city of Chengzhou, lived a man who we know today as Laozi. He was a quiet and learned man who served as a court librarian, hand-copying documents and managing the court's ancient archives. Although he was somewhat reclusive, he attracted many students and disciples and was a respected wise man. This was in the days when Confucius also lived and taught.

One day Confucius went to see Laozi, hoping that the old archivist would share a bit of ancient knowledge and, of course, treat him with respect and deference. Instead, Laozi sharply rebuked Confucius, telling him that his head was too full of rules and regulations and that he would do well to forget all that complexity and simply follow the Dao, the natural way of things. Confucius was stunned. He disappeared for several days, then emerged and told his followers that he had met many impressive people in his life, but none could compare with Laozi, who was "truly like a dragon".

When Laozi was nearing the end of his life, he became tired of the ways of people and decided to head to the western mountains and leave the civilized world for good. But when

Figure 1: stone sculpture of Laozi, at the foot of Mount Qingyuan, Fujian Province, in eastern China.

he reached the western boundary of the Zhou kingdom, a border guard named Yinxi recognized him, and begged him to record some of his wisdom before disappearing into the wilderness. Laozi agreed, and his writings on strips of bamboo later became known as the DDJ. When he was

Figure 2: The Guodian Chu Slips, the earliest known Dao De Jing manuscript, written on bamboo slips, with description and explanation alongside, in white. In Hubei Provincial Museum, China.

finished, he continued on his way and was never seen or heard from again.

For centuries, many Daoists have believed that Laozi, also called Lord Lao, was a manifestation of the Dao itself, conceived when his mother gazed upon a falling star. Not surprisingly, they consider the DDJ to be a divinely revealed document. Scholars and historians, however, agree that regardless of who Laozi was or wasn't, the book we know of today as the DDJ was not the work of a single author, but has been modified and enhanced many times over the centuries. Evidence for this is clear from the half-dozen ancient manuscripts that have been discovered in the last hundred years. The oldest known version of the text, the Guodian Chu Slips, was discovered in 1993 (see Figure 2). Found in a tomb near the town of Guodian, it was written on strips of bamboo in the 4th century BCE but only contained 31 of the 81 chapters. Several other versions have been discovered, most notably the Mawangdui manuscript containing all 81 chapters, written on silk and dating from 200 BCE and unearthed in 1973 (see Figure 3).

On the other hand, some versions of the DDJ have been in general circulation ever since they were originally written in the time of Laozi. These texts, called the "received versions", have been hand-copies many times over the centuries, and often include commentaries. The received versions differ from the more recently discovered manuscripts, which all differ from each other. The contents of individual chapters vary from one manuscript to another, the orders of the chapters change (in some versions the Dao section is placed after the De section), and some verses and entire chapters appear and disappear from one manuscript to the next.[2]

The first known English translation of the DDJ was published by Protestant missionary John Chalmers in 1868 and called *The Speculations on Metaphysics, Polity, and Morality of the 'Old Philosopher' Lau-tsze*. Many other translations followed, and today there are said to be over 250 translations into major Western languages. Some try to remain as faithful as possible to the original Chinese text. Others tend to incorporate the translators' own beliefs and cultural biases, adding words and concepts that never existed in the text of the original DDJ.

道

As we worked on this translation, we wanted to express the DDJ in simple language that anyone can access. This is a book for ordinary people, not scholars. Many DDJ translations have been created by scholars for other scholars, and while we have studied many of them and owe a debt of gratitude to those scholars, we feel that the DDJ's message is simple, practical and universal, and we want everyone to

---

[2] In this book, our starting point is the "consensus version" developed by Bruce R. Linnell and published online as *Dao De Jing: A Minimalist Translation* (www.gutenberg.org/files/49965/49965-h/49965-h.htm). Linnell started with the three highest quality received versions – Wang Bi, Heshang Gong and Fu Yi – and wherever he encountered disagreement among those sources, he simply used the wording that 2 of the 3 sources agreed upon.

have the chance to benefit from it. We try to follow the guidance of Laozi in Chapter 70, who tells us, in his usual elliptical way:

> My words are very easy to understand,
> Very easy to practice.
> In this world, they can't be understood,
> And can't be practiced.

Maybe we can't help you put the DDJ's works into practice in your everyday life, but at least we can help you understand Laozi's words.

It's impossible to do a 100% literal translation of the DDJ. Ordinary modern Chinese is quite different from Western languages, and the language used in this book is even more different. To start with, the DDJ is extremely compact. Its verses have very few connecting words, forcing the reader to think deeply about the verse in order to tease out its underlying meaning or meanings. Some words can, depending on context, serve as nouns, verbs, adjectives or adverbs. Verbs in Chinese generally have no past, present or future tense, nouns have no gender (male/female), and no number (singular/plural). And to make things even more difficult, helpful little words like prepositions and pronouns are often missing entirely.

As a result, translating literally from Chinese to English usually results in gibberish. We've added just enough connecting words so that the sentence makes sense, while still expressing Laozi's thoughts as concisely as possible.

We've also tried really hard to avoid the temptation to add things that weren't already there in order to make the sentence more readable. Whenever we do that (for example, adding a pronoun to a sentence that doesn't have one), we note it in the commentary section.

How many ways are there to translate the DDJ? Here's a short example. The first verse of Chapter 23 simply reads 希言自然. This verse has only three Chinese words, requiring a total of four characters. The first word 希 (xī) means *rare*, 言 (yán) means *speak*, and 自然 (zìrán) means *nature* or *natural*, depending on context. Obviously, "Rare speak nature" or "Rare speak natural" would be terrible English. So, here's how various scholars have translated this three-word verse:

1. Speak little. (Star)
2. Nature's words are few. (our translation)
3. Nature says few words. (Light of Spirit)
4. Infrequent speech is natural. (C. Abbott)
5. To speak little is natural. (Muller)
6. In Nature nothing is eternal. (Flowing Hands)
7. To talk little is natural. (Feng/English)
8. To be of few words is natural. (Stenudd)
9. Nature does not have to insist. (Garafalo)
10. Minimal words are naturally so. (Gutenberg Project)
11. Taciturnity is natural to man. (Goddard)

12. Spare speech and let things be. (Roberts)
13. It is natural to speak only rarely. (Ames/Hall)
14. To be taciturn is the natural way. (Susuki)
15. To be sparse in speech is to be spontaneous. (Eno)
16. To use words but rarely is to be natural. (Lau)
17. Saying no words makes things come about by themselves. (Matsumoto)
18. Less spoken, words speak for themselves naturally. (Wikisource)
19. Abstaining from speech marks him who is obeying the spontaneity of his nature. (Legge)

You can see that these nineteen translations give us at least ten completely different meanings for this line! Also, the three original Chinese words have morphed into anywhere from 2 to 13 words of English, and in last three examples, the translators have added words and meaning that were nowhere to be found in the original.

One of the reasons why translators use so many words is that they often try to nail down, with finality, an exact meaning. But the DDJ is full of ambiguous lines. In fact, it seems that Laozi delighted in putting together conflicting or unexpected words, leaving it up to the reader to figure out his meaning. We have no problem with ambiguity. In some cases, we've been able to translate into English while preserving multiple possible meanings. In other cases, we've had to pick one meaning but have noted other possible meanings in the translation notes (not included in this pocket edition).

That brings us to our final goal: we feel that it's not enough to create a plain English translation; it's just as important to preserve the feeling, the brevity and the rhythm of the original as much as possible. The DDJ's verses are incredibly compact as you've seen from the example above, and they have a rhythmic structure that's often lost or garbled when translated to English. We've tried really hard to preserve those rhythms as much as possible, which sometimes results in English that's not quite grammatically correct but, we hope, captures the essence of the original.

A final note about gender. Chinese is mostly gender-neutral; words are generally not male or female. For example, 人 (rén) means *person* or *people*, not necessarily *man, men, woman* or *women*, and the third-person pronoun 者 (zhě) means *he, she, him, her, them,* or *it,* depending on context. We've maintained this gender neutrality, with just three exceptions. Whenever the word 夫 (fū) is used to mean *men,* this is clearly masculine so we use *men* instead of *people.* When talking about rulers and kings, we use masculine pronouns in keeping with Chinese history. And we use *he, his* or *him* where it would be too awkward (or simply wrong, in the case of Chapter 55) to force the English to be gender neutral.

RESOURCES

We encourage you to try your hand at developing your own translation of the DDJ, or at least digging deeper into translations done by others. Here are some good starting points:

1. Dao De Jing in Clear English, Including a Step by Step Translation, by Jeff Pepper and Xiao Hui Wang (Imagin8 Press, 2018). The same translation as this book, but with an additional 250 pages of translation notes to help you understand the original Chinese.

2. Dao De Jing by Lao Zi: A Minimalist Translation by Bruce R. Linnell, PhD (2015), part of the Gutenberg Project, published online at www.gutenberg.org/files/49965/49965-h/49965-h.htm. It provides spare, almost word-for-word translations, with useful commentary.

3. The Chinese Text Project (http://ctext.org/dao-de-jing#n11636) provides very good online tools for translating the text word by word. Beware their full text translations, however, they are from Legge's 1891 translation and his attempt to make the verses rhyme in English serve only to obscure the meaning and clarity of the original.

4. The Hermetica project (http://hermetica.info) by Bradford Hatcher. He offers a minimalist, word-for-word translation of the DDJ, and his "matrix translation" is an interesting resource for seeing

alternate meanings of each word in the DDJ.

5. <u>The Dao Bums</u> (www.thedaobums.com) is a wonderful online discussion forum for serious students of the DDJ, and includes chapter-by-chapter discussions of the finer points of the text.

6. <u>The Wiktionary</u> (https://en.wiktionary.org/wiki), part of the Wikipedia family of websites, is a useful tool for digging deeper into the meanings of individual Chinese characters.

7. <u>Lao Tzu's Tao Te Ching Translators' Resource</u> (www.taoteching. co.uk) by Arthur W. Hummel, offers a variety of free translators' tools.

8. <u>Google Translate</u> (https://translate.google.com) can be useful, but it gives modern translations which can be quite different from the meanings that the words had 2500 years ago.

ABOUT THE AUTHORS

Jeff Pepper (author) is President and CEO of Imagin8 Press, and has written dozens of books about Chinese language and culture. Over his thirty-five year career he has founded and led several successful computer software firms, including one that became a publicly traded company. He's authored two software related books and was awarded three U.S. software patents.

Dr. Xiao Hui Wang (translator), has an M.S. in Information Science, an M.D. in Medicine, a Ph.D. in Neurobiology and Neuroscience, and 25 years experience in academic and clinical research. She has taught Chinese for over 10 years and has extensive experience in translating Chinese to English and English to Chinese.

Made in the USA
Columbia, SC
26 May 2021

38540880R00063